Spiritual Leadership in the Missional Church

A Systems Approach to Leadership as Cultivation

Nigel Rooms

Leader, Partnership for Missional Church UK,
Church Mission Society and Associate Priest,
St Peter's, Braunstone Park, Diocese of Leicester

Patrick Keifert

President and Director of Consulting,
Church Innovations Institute, USA

GROVE BOOKS LIMITED
RIDLEY HALL RD CAMBRIDGE CB3 9HU

Contents

Preface

We have written this book as a kind of sequel to our 2014 booklet in the Grove Pastoral series 'Forming the Missional Church' (Grove Pastoral booklet P139). It answers the question begged by that book of what kind of leadership is required in missional churches. Chapters one to three are primarily Nigel's work and chapters four to six are Pat's.

CPAS is an Anglican evangelical mission agency working mainly in the UK and Republic of Ireland. We enable churches to help every person hear and discover the good news of Jesus Christ. Our vision is to see effective, Christ-like leaders at all levels in our churches: men, women and young people who point others to Jesus. Good leadership is key to church growth and that is why we are investing all our energy in developing leaders.
www.cpas.org.uk.

Copyright © Nigel Rooms and Patrick Keifert 2019

First Impression October 2019
ISSN 2041-0972
ISBN 978 1 78827 101 1

Introduction

I am a gardener; my father taught me most of what I know when I was growing up and I have continued to learn how to grow most of the vegetables we eat at home on my allotment. This book connects leadership with organic cultivation metaphors following Alan Roxburgh's lead.[1] A spiritual leader in church terms is, in our approach to being missional, the cultivator of the environment.[2] Given the right environment the local church, as a living organism, can flourish, die and live again, sometimes simultaneously.

In contrast, we have lived through a technical age steeped in mechanical metaphors with leaders asking for a toolkit to apply to their churches. They use these words unconsciously and at the same time betray a modernist mind-set that treats human organizations as if they were a machine to be fixed.

As a gardener I know several things:

- I cannot make plants grow—God does this in the most amazing, beautiful ways. The worst thing I can do, having planted a seed which has not immediately germinated, is to dig it up to check if it is growing!

- I can create a healthier environment for growth. I took on a new plot recently and spent all winter double-digging it to remove the weeds and fertilize it.

- What I allow and disallow across the boundary of the land is vital. We have caterpillars, slugs, beetles, pigeons, pheasants, rabbits, foxes and squirrels who all want to share my produce. And without good inputs like well-rotted, wormy manure there will be sparse pickings.

- The conditions vary for growth each year in the UK; some years are very dry, others very wet. Preparing for and living with such tension is part of the task. I often choose several varieties of a plant that generally means I get a good crop from one or two of them.

This book is about leadership as cultivation. We are going to understand churches as living organisms and therefore take a systems approach to understand how to work with them for their flourishing. We will examine two versions of systems theory and discern their usefulness for us. We will think about how the leader's task is holding both the purpose and boundary of the system and the implications of that for their self-definition and identity formation (an ultimately spiritual task). Finally, we will address the importance of leaders holding irreconcilable opposites in tension for the sake of the whole system.

Most of this material, in our experience, is not taught in theological colleges or in leadership development courses. We think that in a missional church leaders need to be able to create the right emotional and spiritual field in which the congregation can flourish—just like a good gardener.

A Systems Approach to Church Life: Understanding the Ecology

The 'porous bounded organism' is a root metaphor which upholds a way of thinking about human life both as individuals and communities.[3] Organic life is made up of individual cells which are complex systems of interacting proteins, lipids and nucleic acids. All living cells allow input and output across their semi-permeable boundary. If they cease to be permeable to their outside environment they quickly die.

We can easily scale up the metaphor to individual human beings, contained as we are within skin-covered bodies, and interacting with one another in creating distinct groups and organizations with boundaries. The cell, the body, the human group are all therefore types of system. What is called 'systems thinking' then arises: treating an organized group of people, like a local church, as a living, organic system.

In a church of just 50 people there are 1,225 potential relationships. In one of 100 it becomes 4,950. Mapping those relationships individually would be a massive task, particularly if we understood them as working in a cause and effect linear fashion from A to B. It is better to understand the whole as a living system and treat it as such.

Every person is a system in themselves, and is potentially related to everyone else in the wider systems they participate in. In this theory the individuals involved both retain their individuality and are deeply affected by all the others in the system. What matters then is their *position* in the system rather than the nature of what and who they are. This is a non-linear way of thinking about organizations and connects deeply with my theological anthropology. I believe that human beings, made in the image of the triune God who is a community of three in one, are also *beings in communion*. That is, the individual person cannot be separated from the community, but their individuality must always be safeguarded. Stanley Grenz quotes the Orthodox theologian John Zizioulas as saying,

> The person cannot exist without communion; but every form of communion which denies or suppresses the person is inadmissible.[4]

There are many ways to theorize and think about organizations as systems. We are going to present the bare bones of two of them in this chapter as a way of helping leaders understand the ecology of the local church, so that they can cultivate the environment for maximum flourishing.

The first is family systems theory, arising from studying human nuclear and extended families in a therapeutic and psychotherapeutic manner. The second is open systems theory, founded by Kurt Lewin and others after WWII from work they did on human group dynamics (now known as human or group relations).[5]

Family Systems Theory

All one needs to know at a basic level about this is found in Edwin Friedman's *Generation to Generation: Family Process in Church and Synagogue*.[6] My short summary here is heavily dependent on that book.

Four out of the five basic interrelated concepts of the theory are worth rehearsing here.[7]

The Identified or Designated Patient
Where there is stress, anxiety or some other pathology in a human system, it tends to surface and be represented by one individual in the system. This is the identified or designated patient—they become like a lightning rod for the negative energy in the system. When providing support and help to the system they are *most expressly not* the person to focus on or even remove to make things better. Rather, the whole system needs to be treated to some new input or way of working which changes all the relationships and especially those of the designated patient. In major church bodies in the UK there has been at least 1% decline (or more) in membership every year for the last fifty or so years. No initiative has reversed this trend and the resultant systems are highly anxious and treated pathologically. The leaders, most especially the ordained local clergy, become the designated patient in the system. They are trained ever more highly and expensively, driven ever harder to produce results and often discarded when they are burnt out or seen not to be productive. Other things need to happen than focusing ever more closely on the clergy, though this is not to say that leadership is unimportant (as we shall see in chapters three and four).

Homeostasis or Autopoiesis
There is a basic rule of human organizations that is described by this theory (which it shares with open systems theory). As stated by Friedman it is:

> ...the tendency of any set of relationships to strive perpetually, in self-corrective ways, to preserve the organizing principles of its existence.[8]

To put it another way, no matter what changes (or initiatives) are introduced to the system it adjusts itself back to the balanced *status quo* or equilibrium. We have here a more sophisticated way of saying the famous line attributed (perhaps falsely) to Peter Drucker, 'Culture eats strategy for breakfast.' As clergy come and go it is very hard to change the core of what happens in a local church over the very long term and to make any change permanent beyond what any particular (often charismatic) individual brings. Systems theory tells us firmly that change does not happen in straight lines from point A to point B. Human relations in groups simply do not work like that. In creating missional churches, we work with a theory of change from Everett Rogers called *diffusion of innovations* which is much more like the path of a sailboat tacking this way and that to find the wind.[9]

Self-differentiation

We are going to fully address this concept in chapter four so here I will only say that self-differentiation according to Friedman is 'the capacity to be an "I" *while remaining connected.*'[10]

It is definitely not about autonomy and narcissism, hence my emphasis above. It is about how we maintain a (relatively) non-anxious presence in the midst of conflict, crisis and difficulty and remain properly connected into the system without fighting it, fusing with it or fleeing from it.[11] It is a deeply spiritual task.

Triangulation

This is an extension of *homeostasis* in that it operates under this law:

> …when any two parts of a system become uncomfortable with one another, they will 'triangle in' or focus upon a third person, or issue, as a way of stabilizing their own relationship with one another.[12]

Most leaders are familiar with this phenomenon. I know I have been caught in it unawares many times and probably always will be. Having an awareness radar for it really helps and staying in touch responsibly with each of the protagonists while not trying to fix their relationship with each other is usually helpful.

Family systems theory is the basis of many conflict resolution approaches to local church systems, and as such is incredibly useful.[13] But it also has its limitation, two of which are mentioned here. There is evidence that focusing on just the family system and developing healthy ways of dealing with conflict within the system actually reduces the overall level of what we can call good and necessary missional conflict over the longer term. And that may indeed lead to the second, perhaps more important, issue which is that family systems are difficult to *join*. They have a thick boundary and in our contemporary society are easily privatized by the public world. This is why we need to add in an understanding of open systems theory.

Open Systems Theory

Here we return fully to the living organism metaphor as described by Vega Roberts in an important introductory chapter of hers.[14] An open system takes in inputs across its boundary, and there are outputs which leave (see diagram below). There is some transformation or conversion of the inputs to the outputs within the system.[15] It is the input and output across the boundary that keeps the system alive.

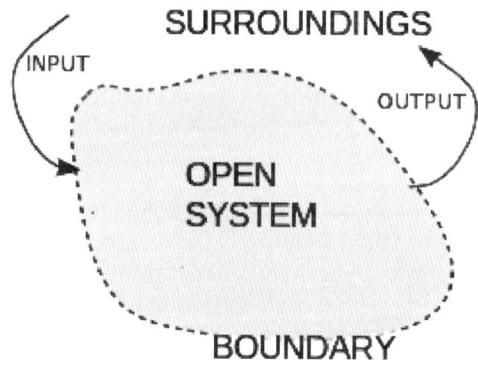

The first thing to note here is that the resources for the future of the system are *without* it. They exist in the surrounding environment. This is why context is key, and theologically, why the church is at its best when focused on its public world in the wider community. Many Anglicans instinctively know this and many non-Anglicans have come to realize this in recent years, for example in the *New Parish* movement.[16] There is good research showing no correlation between how much financial resource a church has and its future. Rather, the local church is dependent on the God *who so loved the world that…*and not on its internal reserves. God did not send Jesus primarily for the church but for the world and the Holy Spirit continues that work always and everywhere.

The boundary of any church system has therefore to be properly porous to the world around it, and the system itself has to be prepared to be changed by the inputs that will come from it as well as expecting them to transform in the process. In missional church thinking the primary or root metaphor for church, *a company of strangers*, following Parker Palmer, is preferable over the fairly ubiquitous (in the authors' experience) metaphor of church as *family*. There are more complex reasons for this but the main one is that welcoming the stranger will always change us, and that is what keeps us alive in our church system.[17]

Of course, human organizations are not like a single cell; they are much more like a body which is made up of many subsystems within an overall function which serves the whole. This takes us to the next important idea in open systems theory—that of the primary task or purpose of the system, 'the task it must perform if it is to survive.'[18]

It does not take much reflection to realize that this is not easy to agree on in a local church or indeed in any complex human organization, not least because the various subsystems (*eg* children's work, choir, social events etc) will all have slightly different tasks which serve the whole. However, 'Where the primary task is defined too narrowly, or in terms of member's needs, the survival of the organization becomes precarious.'[19] We will return to the importance of discerning and holding to the primary task in the next chapter when we also focus on the importance of the leader attending to the boundary of the system.

A final point here is about the outputs of the open system. Output is defined as the action of the system across the boundary. This eventually results in outcomes that are the effect or impact of that action in the system's surroundings (not shown in the diagram above). We are used in church bodies to measuring output in our mechanistic understanding of how we think church works, but rarely investigate outcome or impact. Data from churches in the UK shows that they rarely act in public as a community in the name of the church. They have little impact and many citizens do not know they even exist. Focusing mostly on the outputs of church growth in numbers and financial giving is unlikely to change this situation.

I have a dream that one day a person could walk down the street in any city, town or village and half of the people they met with could tell a story about the impact the local church is making with their community. I have a dream…

3 The Leader at the Boundary

In this chapter we pick up and develop an idea from open systems theory about where leadership is best positioned. Rather than being in a hierarchical position above the system, this theory states leaders are most effectively *located at the boundary*. Roberts comments:

> It is only from this position that they [leaders] can carry out their function of relating what is inside to what is outside the system. This includes being clear about the primary task, attending to the flow of information across the boundary, ensuring the system has the resources it needs to perform its task, and monitoring that this task continues to relate to the requirements of…the external environment.[20]

I spent several years in partnership with the Grubb Institute (which unfortunately no longer exists) using these ideas and working with clergy on their leadership task in an experiential learning environment. I learnt many things there, but perhaps the most sobering was the way in which for many clergy the system—*ie* the human inside of the local church—became all-pervasive so that they lost both a sense of self separate from the system (their 'I'), and the ability to see and understand the wider context in the community. In other words, they were unable to maintain a position at the boundary but were subsumed by the church.

Perhaps it feels much safer in what missiologist and anthropologist Paul Hiebert[21] calls a 'bounded set' (to draw on a comparative idea to open systems from mathematical set theory).[22] However, as we have seen, if the system has an impervious boundary it is wont to die. A centred set, in Hiebert's terms, is much healthier as a missionary enterprise, and this is how we now think of missional churches. They are centred on joining in with the activity of God (like the nucleus of the cell) and the people are variously moving towards or away from that centre. Christian community is always being formed around what God is up to. At some point there is a boundary, but it is often hard to tell exactly where it is.

The leader (read cultivator) is located therefore at this rather fuzzy, even messy, boundary. There are three important tasks implied by this location.

Gaining a Balcony View

Getting up on the balcony is a metaphor for leadership at the boundary from Ron Heifetz.[23] He describes the day-to-day experience of working in an organization or system as like being on a dance floor. It is really hard to gain a sense of what is going on from a ground-level position. However, getting up to the balcony gives the observer a whole new perspective, seeing patterns, changes and movements (and this is not the same as a traditional hierarchical position above the system). The key skill, says Heifetz, is being able to be *simultaneously* on the dance floor and the balcony. This can only be learned by experience and is actually what great anthropologists (and, in my view, great priests as boundary / liminal people) have always been able to do. The anthropologists call their key skill *participant observation.* They argue interminably as to whether it is actually possible, but they stick to the need to be both present within and objectively observing whatever people group they are studying.

Unfortunately, many clergy are trained in gaining either an aeroplane view (at 35,000ft) or at best a helicopter view (at say 500ft). To the airline passenger the broad outline of what is below can be discerned, the truly big picture. A helicopter view might be thought of as being better—contours are clearer and a few patterns can emerge but, in some ways, this can be even more dangerous since, to quote Alfred Korzybski (1879–1950), 'The map is not the territory.' We need the balcony view, close enough to see real people with names and faces dancing together or being wallflowers in the corner, distant enough not to be simply dazzled and confused by the complexity of what is happening.

Being a spiritual leader is so often about seeing differently

Being a spiritual leader, therefore, is so often about seeing, seeing differently or, as Michael Paterson has put it, gaining *visio divina.*[24] I have always loved the humour in John 9 where somehow the religious professionals (like me) are not able to see, unlike the poor man who could not, but now can. Professor John Hull, my doctoral supervisor, was physically blind but saw me in several ways I never imagined possible.

Another way of putting this is paying attention, or truly attending. The best waiters in restaurants (like sports referees) are almost invisible. They are able to notice when you need them and when you do not. They clear the plates at just the right time, not too soon and not too late. How do they do that? By paying attention—waiting, in the fullest sense of that word.

And what to do with this divine sight—or perhaps a better word is *insight*— that is borne of attending on the balcony? The simple answer is directing others' attention to what the leader has noticed too. When a God moment happens, when someone moves towards the centre, or crosses the porous boundary and it is spotted, can the leader help those making the move to see what is happening too? Can the story be told in its fine detail so that it might encourage everyone and be repeated? These are the skills of the insightful spiritual leader who helps people to notice what God is up to so others can join in too.

Creating a Holding Tank

In some depictions of the open systems theory diagram there is a level of turbulence or transformation that occurs within the porous boundary of the system as the inputs become outputs. This requires energy and an amount of disturbance and even conflict within the system. A bit like cooking a cake, it is no good if the oven temperature is too low (soggy bottom) or too high (King Alfred and the peasant's cakes). Church systems also require a proper level of disturbance and good, healthy conflict if they are going to be alive, change and grow.

Church systems require a proper level of disturbance if they are going to grow

However, Heifetz also tells us that the leader's task is to create a safe enough container or holding tank from the boundaries of the system for this conflict to do its work, for it to be geared into missional activity and not just become destructive. There is a much longer history behind this approach, particularly from developmental psychology in childhood, following the work of Donald Winnicott (1896–1971). His research showed how a mother provides containment, a holding environment for the messiness of infanthood. The mother crafts the emotional space for play and creativity and therefore learning to happen—a good enough space for emotional growth and maturity to emerge.

We will say more about the grounding of the skill of generating a holding tank in the next chapter on the individual leader and their spiritual life, but how to create such an environment? Heifetz states that the rules will be context dependent, and gives some pointers.[25] However, easier to remember is the three Ts, a kind of mantra I also learnt from the Grubb Institute: *time, task and territory.*

Have you ever been to a different kind of church from your own and it is clear that the worship might go on for a long *time*, but you have no idea when it will end? It does not feel particularly safe. Being clear always about start and end times of any event or discernment, particularly if it is controversial, will create a feeling of safety and containment. Time boundaries really matter.

Sticking to the *task* in any meeting and being clear about its purpose (which will normally be related to the primary task—see next section) will mean that distractions and subversions will be disallowed and the group can be brought gently back to the task in hand.

Territory is often ignored in organizations but it is also key to a safe environment where good and effective work can be done. For instance, how many times have I turned up at a training event where the chairs are arranged in rows facing the front. People need to be able to see some other people's faces in the room if they are to trust one another and not be given the impression that the person at the front knows everything.

Contracting all these things either before an event or at the start sets the correct boundaries (a further example would be confidentiality) and the work can proceed effectively.

Discerning the Primary Task

Of fundamental significance in open systems theory is the *primary task* or *purpose* of the system—this is defined, as we have seen in the previous chapter, as 'the task it must perform if it is to survive.' In other places this would be called the vision or the mission of the organization. We also noted that where the primary task is defined too narrowly, or in terms of members' needs, the survival of the organization becomes precarious. We can see, therefore, that understanding the purpose of the church as growth in numbers is defining a primary task *internally*. A porous church will be looking to create a vision that can be owned by

For a local church to survive, its primary task must be connected with its immediate environment

those inside *and outside* of its boundary (and such a vision will then endure beyond any individual leader / clergyperson). Open systems theory suggests therefore that for a local church to survive *its primary task must be connected in transformative ways with its immediate environment*. I suggest that any great vision statement for a local church will involve reframing the wider biblical story of God's mission in relation to the *here and now* of what God is up to at this particular place and time.

Defining the primary task is always complex, since in any organization there will be the *normative, existential* and *phenomenal* primary tasks.[26] The normative primary task is that espoused by the organization in its public face, whereas this is often translated into an existential primary task by the various actors within the system (what we think we are doing) and finally a phenomenal primary task may emerge (how we actually behave), however unconscious that behaviour might be. A local church might desire to grow in numbers, so develops a fresh welcoming team, yet still struggles to retain newcomers.

We emphasize here, then, with Roberts that 'When a group does not seek to know its primary task...there is likely to emerge either dismemberment of the group, or the emergence of some other primary task unrelated [to the original].'[27] This sounds familiar to me. The leader at the boundary enables the whole system to discern its primary task (which often takes years of hard work, experiment and learning from failure) so that the vision then is owned and embodied by the congregation. New leaders come to join in with this ongoing vision (*and* it is never finally fixed, but always under review) rather than creating a new one of their own.

Finding a God-centred Self-definition

4

In this chapter we explore the ultimately spiritual task of seeking a God-centred self-definition, adding in the perspective of God to Friedman's concept of self-definition. Seeking a God-centred self-definition, a clear sense of who you are within God's call, provides the most powerful place for spiritual leadership. It is about the combination of vocation, which perhaps comes first, and then identity. We gain such a self-definition through living out a realistic rule of life.

Good leaders need to be a relatively non-anxious presence in the midst of the turbulent transformations that occur between inputs and outputs within the open system of the missional church. It is the spiritual leader who creates a holding environment for attending, asserting, agreeing and acting together in high levels of complexity (and even chaos) as the missional temperature is raised in the local congregation. To achieve this, they need regular (usually daily, weekly, monthly and annual) spiritual practices which, over time, form a grounded spiritual rhythm in the subject. In short, without regular spiritual practices for providing a clear sense of self-definition, *complexity, chaos and, hence, anxiety rule*. Rather than facilitating a relatively safe holding environment for the local church, the leader gets lost in what we call the anxiety of incumbentism—they are forever busy without ever achieving very much.[28]

> **Seeking a God-centred self-definition is the most practical aspect of spiritual leadership**

Ironically, the professionalization of clergy education has focused on an increasing number of specialized subject-matters of ministry, many of which might take clergy away from what they discern as the primary task. In contrast, we follow the theory of leadership as self-differentiation rather than focusing on skill in various ministerial expert functions. Seeking a God-centred self-definition is the most practical, and at the same time most spiritual, aspect of spiritual leadership.

Relating to God

By emphasizing the practical importance of relating to God the Trinity in prayer, we are challenging how the spiritual dimension of life in contemporary Western societies is valued only as private and esoteric, irrelevant to the public (ordinary and practical). We have not the space to argue fully that when we pray, we pray in public (even when the door is closed (Matt 6.6)) but we will take it to be true. Here we connect the sacred and secular, conjoin contemplation and action (following Richard Rohr) and go into the desert, not to escape from people, but to find them in God (Thomas Merton). Rather than understanding spiritual practices as purely private and esoteric, we understand them to include the capacity to step back and gain the larger picture of life and ministry, to see the balcony view, as we have called it. This is because prayer, at root, is also about paying attention—can we stay still enough, for long enough, away from the next email/phone call/interruption, to notice the movement of God in us? And remember, this stillness can be found for some in physical activity such as walking, running, swimming, cycling etc.

Prayer, at root, is about paying attention, and to notice the movement of God in us

Within some traditions, creating such a rhythm of spiritual practices is called a rule of life, borrowing language from the long history of religious communities going back to the Rule of St Benedict in the sixth century. It is worth noting that Benedict created his rule at the end of the Roman Empire—a complex, chaotic and anxiety-inducing time not unlike our own. Others prefer to focus less on the image of rule by exploring the multiple practices that the Christian tradition offers the contemporary spiritual leader. Whether the emphasis be on one rule of life or the exploration of multiple spiritual practices, the focus and outcome of these spiritual practices is a God-centred self-definition.

Relationship within the Trinity

As Christian spiritual leaders, the centre of these spiritual practices is the movement within the life of the triune God which we are seeking to pay attention to first in ourselves, then in God's people as well as in the world. In this way we participate in the *missio Dei*. Perhaps the most radical and liberating moment for Christian leaders is encountering the multiple relationships available within the Trinity. This encounter liberates us from the notion that we are autonomous beings who have rejected any rule or direction from another. We can only resolve the impasse between the rock of self-rule and the hard place of another's rule by participating in the life of the Trinity. Here we encounter life before the irreducible other that is being in communion with our own being, grounded as it is in the *imago Dei*. Released from the prison of the choice between a fundamentalist self which is alone, or unquestioning submission to the rule of the other, the Christian experiences the freedom of life within the community of love. When the Christian dwells within this life and seeks a self-definition within this being as communion, they discover both self-definition and the ability to stay in touch with others even in the midst of conflict and chaos.

At the heart of this journey is the cross. In the cross the Christian spiritual leader brings their doubt, guilt, shame, fear, failure, even death—and receives faith, forgiveness, delight, courage, and life within the challenges of each day. They are free to risk the dangerous and exciting work of cultivating an environment that takes on contemporary life within our complex world and to return, through their spiritual practice, to seek this liberating self-definition within the Trinity.

Seeking such a God-centred self-definition relieves the contemporary spiritual leader from the temptation to be the spiritual hero/warrior or become the exhausted secular activist/leader. As personal, and at times deeply private, as spiritual practices might be, they emit a public persona as well, one transparent to life under the cross within the life of the Trinity. Such leaders have sufficient sense of self and capacity to stay in touch with others and to invite those others into the relatively safer holding environment that local Christian communities need to flourish in this new missional era.

Creating a Rule of Life

The question remains, how do we create a suitable rule of life for ourselves (even if we do not call it that)? There are several good books on this subject, including at least one in the Grove Spirituality series.[29] Here is our take on the subject that we hope might add something to that literature for you, the reader.

First, we want to say that *everyone has a rule of life*. Some are *implicit*, hidden within our lives, and some are *explicit*, and can be articulated by the holder of the rule. The problem with a purely implicit, unarticulated rule is that our good intentions often become eroded over time by the constant and insistent demands of leadership. Some years ago, Nigel worked with a clergyperson who had essentially stopped attending to any spiritual practice and was responding to urgent emails in the gaps in the day from early in the morning until late at night. Any Bible reading, reflection and prayer that was going on was focused on delivering the church's worship in a utilitarian manner. Needless to say,

Everyone has a rule of life; some are implicit and some are explicit

both the ministry and the personal life of the leader were suffering greatly. After agreeing a simple rule banning emails for twelve hours from 9pm to 9am, alongside attending to the person's chosen life-giving spiritual practice (purely for its own sake) for some of that space, within six months we had a different human being and spiritual leader altogether.

Some people can carry their rule or rhythm of spiritual practice with them in their hearts and articulate it when asked. For others, writing it down or drawing it in pictures or using an image really helps. Some rules focus solely on the prayer and spiritual life of the person, but in fact it can be incredibly helpful to include some kind of 360 degree view as well. Where and how is time allocated for close and more distant family relationships, building friendships for their own sake, relaxation, life outside of ministry, physical recreation etc?

The focus in a rule of life, as we have seen, is on time and its rhythms. We need daily, weekly, monthly, annual and longer time frames (*eg* the seven/ten year sabbatical cycle. Placed all together there is a creative interplay and correction/accountability between the various practices. For instance, the extended time on an annual retreat gives a chance to review the more frequent practices, try out new ones and enhance the whole.

A good rule of life is often created with a trusted other. In fact, we believe it is very hard to sustain life as a Christian leader in today's world without a good spiritual director and a peer support group where everyone can level with each other and say exactly how they are without judgment (regular pastoral supervision would help too but this is a separate subject). Most important, though, is spiritual direction. Nigel has written elsewhere about

Spiritual practice is about paying attention to the movement and activity of God

the relationship of spiritual direction to joining in the mission of God since, as we have noted, spiritual practice is about paying attention to the movement and activity of God.[30] This occurs both in the spiritual-direction room, and at the macro scale in the missional church.

Our experience of working with Christian leaders and clergy around the country is that very many are familiar with the idea of having a rule of life, but rather fewer actually keep one. We wonder why this might be. Here we think the Pareto principle or the 80/20 rule might helpfully apply. No-one who lives outside of a bounded religious community, we believe, can keep their rule 100% of the time. The question is, if we are to live by grace, not law, how much should we be able to live by our rule? We suggest 80% of the time or more would be a good rule of thumb. Some days it just will not work out. However, if we *cannot make it 80%* of the time we suggest that *it is the wrong rule.* It needs adjusting so it can be kept up for around 80% of the time. A basic principle of prayer is, 'Pray as you can, not as you cannot.' If five minutes a day with God is possible, spend five minutes of at least 80% of days with God. Something will change and then a further desire to be grounded in the life of the Trinity might emerge.

In closing this chapter, we suggest that missional church is more than anything about *awakening desire* for participating in the overflow of God's love, which is present in every moment. Each individual's journey into that love is unique. What we are inviting you to do is to ask, 'How is your desire for the triune

However, spiritual leaders sense that some of the difficulties facing local churches are more adaptive and complex. Usually, after trying various quick fixes, the spiritual leaders conclude these difficulties are not problems to be solved. Spiritual leadership senses that the difficulties being faced are life or death matters, and they also know they do not have easy answers. No matter how they frame the difficulty as a problem to be solved, the character of the difficulties is not helpfully comprehended. We call these difficulties, following the work of Heifetz cited earlier, 'adaptive challenges.'

The classic example here is children and young people. Many churches today would cite this as their number one problem. They simply do not have them and they know they need them for their future. It might be counterintuitive but in fact this problem is a technical one. There are plenty of off-the-shelf fixes for gaining children and young people in church. The issue is that when they arrive they are disruptive of the *status quo*, lots of versions of 'shushing' take place and they are unconsciously frozen out over time. We suggest there is a deeper adaptive challenge to be faced here, that is at root an unresolvable polarity . This is a theme to which we will return.

We invite spiritual leaders, while understanding themselves as cultivators of the environment, to learn to discern certain difficulties as polarities to be managed rather than problems to be solved. The core text here is by Barry Johnson and we are dependent for much of the rest of this chapter on his work.[33]

Learn to discern certain difficulties as polarities to be managed rather than problems to be solved

Managing Polarities

Polarities exist all around us in everyday life. Breathing is a perfect example. Breathing is made up of two poles that are clear opposites but interdependent: inhaling and exhaling. When one needs to inhale, it is important not to exhale, and *vice versa*. The one pulls oxygenated air into the lungs; the other expels carbon-dioxide-rich air. Too much of either kills. Not enough of both also kills. This polarity needs to be managed. To be sure, in most everyday circumstances the body manages this polarity very well. Most of the time, we do not think about it. Both poles are essential for life even if they are polar opposites.

Polarities can be diagrammatically represented by a four-quadrant grid or map. The two poles are separated horizontally and the positive and negative effects of both poles are the vertical axis. Polarities are not problems to be solved but poles to be managed, like breathing. The problem is never actually solved. Indeed, only by managing the poles can life go on. That life is an infinite loop around the four quadrants.

In their very helpful book, *Managing Polarities in Congregations: Eight Keys for Thriving Faith Communities*, Roy Oswald and Barry Johnson note eight common polarities to be managed in churches.[34] One very common complex and conflicted polarity is given as an example here.

In this instance a new spiritual leader had received the message from the call committee (we might refer to the vacancy document or parish profile) that the congregation was dying because it had no outreach ministry. The congregation was getting smaller because it was turning in on itself. More and more of the previous spiritual leader's time and that of others had been spent on the maintenance of the ongoing gathered community that continued to find issues to fight about, without end. The outcome of each fight was fewer people to worship or fight. Those calling the new spiritual leader named this focus as the problem of 'inreach.' They called their new spiritual leader to focus on outreach, thus ensuring a future.

The new spiritual leader had successfully grown a church-based social ministry to street people in another part of the same city in which the calling congregation was. Since two members of the congregation already participated in this outreach ministry, they were sure the fresh spiritual leader could grow their local church in the same way. She, together with them, could solve the problem of inreach.

After five years of growing an outreach ministry sponsored by the congregation, a significant group of persons were very committed to the ministry. The leader was often engaged with them in the very effective outreach ministry. However, Sunday worship, children and youth ministry continued to decline in numbers of participants and leaders. Older members and their descendants complained bitterly about the church not caring about them. They either became vocal opponents of outreach ministry or simply left the congregation. The leader and the supporters of outreach ministry became more convinced that the only future was to develop outside financial resources for their growing outreach ministry. They put more and more energy into developing the outreach ministry, simply declaring that those who left, or stayed and complained, were representing the past and would 'soon pass away.'

Oswald and Johnson effectively show that this is not a problem to solve but a polarity to be managed, the two poles that are opposite being: inreach and outreach. A local church cannot survive without both poles being strengthened. Rather than focusing on the negatives of each pole, spiritual leadership needs to recognize the reality of negative outcomes to both poles, and manage the system to the positive outcomes of each pole. It is an important principle in polarity management that leaders attempt to manage the polarity upwards on the four quadrant grid, so more of the activity is in the upper, positive quadrants.

Here a useful learning exercise for the reader would be to make your own version of the polarity map of inreach/outreach. This issue is familiar in most churches and filling in the grid should be instructive.

Balancing Belonging and Bridging

In the years since learning from Oswald and Johnson, I have found another, closely related, polarity to be managed. It is named by two different sociologists in two different ways but it describes the same sociological phenomenon. Robert Wuthnow names the polarity as the sociology of joining *vs* belonging. Robert Putnam names the polarity as the sociology of bonding and bridging. Any successful local church must manage these polarities. It is the key to the dilemma presented by children and young people in our original example, or in fact any newcomers to church who look and act differently from the current membership.

Again, think of it in diagrammatic form. On the left-hand pole place the sociology of bonding and belonging. On this pole the primary purpose of all behaviour is to form strong loyalty and corporate identification among those who are regularly gathered in the local church. On the right-hand pole place the sociology of bridging and joining. On this pole the primary purpose of all behaviour is to create the trust necessary among strangers who do not share all the values and identification of those who regularly gather in the local church. A comparison with our understanding of churches as open systems is now available.

One group tends to focus on the negatives of the other as the problem

However, as in all polarities to be managed, one group tends to focus on the negatives of the other pole as the problem. Those primarily committed to belonging and bonding see the negative outcomes of joining and bridging—these children and young people disturb the tranquillity and beauty of Sunday worship! Those primarily committed to joining and bridging focus on the negative outcomes of belonging and bonding—the congregation are fuddy-duddy stick-in-the-muds! They each see the other pole as a problem to be solved.

Further ethnographic study has identified a similar phenomenon in many organizations and groups in contemporary post-industrial societies. It shows that those focused on the belonging and bonding pole have loyalty and fidelity to the group as their highest moral virtue. Those focused on the bridging and joining pole have the establishing of trust among strangers as their highest moral virtue. The research demonstrates that thriving communities and groups require both sets of virtues and need them in abundance.

The spiritual leader can use polarity management to strengthen the positives of both poles as noted above. This is costly, of course, since the leader will be eternally caught (even crucified?) between the two poles. The spiritual leader lives in the infinite loop of recognizing both the positive and negative outcomes of each pole and framing the difficulty not as a problem to be solved but a polarity to be managed. Like inhaling and exhaling, local churches that strengthen both belonging and bonding activities and joining and bridging activities breathe new life into themselves. They live through the leadership of the Holy Spirit into God's preferred and promised future for them.

Conclusion

6

We have invited spiritual leaders to understand themselves as cultivators of the rich soil of the local church within the life of the Trinity. We now summarize these insights into an acronym: ARCH. An arch takes us from one place to another.

Attending

Perhaps the most critical task of a spiritual leader is, like a great waiter in a restaurant, attending; attending to the field of action both within the local church and the many publics it serves (*ie* those different cultures and contexts it needs to relate to in the public sphere). Attending as we understand it includes the emotional field that forms all human action in community, the relationships and energies that make up human action within a local church and those publics. This includes not only the personal dynamics, organizational systems and economic and political givens, but most importantly the deep cultural values and spiritual energies—both good and bad, holy and profane.

Reframing

The spiritual leader attends to the work of the Holy Spirit by both spending regular time in their own work of developing a God-centred self-definition, and by inviting the local church (and its many publics) to participate in what God is up to. This work requires a reframing of the traditional narratives of local church in the wider biblical story of God's mission and kingdom.

The spiritual leader begins by dwelling in the word of God in daily practices that lead to their own reframing and renewal in God's call to them. The spiritual leader continues this reframing work by inviting the local church and its other publics into such dwelling in the Scriptures. This often takes the shape of interpreting the work of these groups within the biblical narrative.

One of the most effective spiritual leaders with whom I worked described his work as a 'secretary'! I asked him how he led a local church through many massive changes (and significant growth) in its desire to participate in God's mission within its local contexts. He spoke of managing the polarity of those who were dedicated to the bonding and belonging pole with that of the joiners and bridge builders by effectively being their secretary.

When I asked him about this image, he said he never chaired a parish council (or any other church meeting) but functioned as the secretary, the one who took the minutes of their meetings, decisions and actions. As secretary he attended to the main thing in their very complex, chaotic and often conflicted meetings: decisions, and actions. He kept them focused by interpreting their work within the biblical narrative as it worked itself out in their lives.

Cultivating

Cultivating has been the main focus of this book. We have invited spiritual leaders to attend to the energies of the local church and the publics they serve. When the spiritual leader attends to these energies, they also are attending to forces that work for good (and ill). Another way of speaking of spiritual energies is speaking of power, the ability to focus the energy to achieve things. By attending to these, they focus on the powers that be, both evil and holy. In the face of often overwhelming forces, principalities and powers that seek to kill rather than give life, the spiritual leader focuses on the work of God, God's mission in their local church and the publics it serves. Rather than look at these with the question, 'What the hell is going on here?' we invite them to look with the question, 'What in heaven's name is going on here?' We encourage the spiritual leader to take seriously the promise of the Holy Spirit to lead their community into God's preferred and promised future. In short, cultivate the rich soil of life in the triune God.

Holding

Last, but hardly least, the essential task of the spiritual leader as cultivator of the rich soil of life in the triune God—is that of holding; holding the local church and its publics in a relatively safe environment for discerning God's preferred and promised future.

In order for the spiritual leader to exercise leadership that creates and sustains such holding environments, we have argued that undertaking regular spiritual practices out of a rule of life is the most powerful and practical action they can take. Such a rule of life grounds the spiritual leader in a God-centred self-definition so that they can provide that crucial, appropriate, non-anxious presence as they lead the Christian community. Such presence creates the emotional and spiritual field which holds the disciples of Christ as they discern and act to form Christian community within God's mission in God's beloved world.

Notes

1. Alan J Roxburgh and Fred Romanuk, *The Missional Leader: Equipping your Church to Reach a Changing World* (San Francisco, CA: Jossey Bass, 2006) p 152.

2. Missional denotes the 'being' or formation of a church within God's mission, the *missio Dei*. Everything the church is and does is focused on joining in what God is up to—collaborating with the creator as good gardeners also do. See also our Grove booklet, *Forming the Missional Church* (Grove Pastoral booklet P139).

3. Barry Palmer, 'The Tavistock Paradigm, Inside, Outside and Beyond' in Robert Hinshelwood and Marco Chiesa (eds), *Organisations, Anxieties and Defences: Towards a Psychoanalytic Social Psychology* (London: Routledge, Taylor and Francis, 2002).

4. Stanley Grenz, *The Social God and the Relational Self: A Trinitarian Theology of the* Imago Dei (Louisville, KY: Westminster John Knox, 2001) p 53. On theological anthropology see also my chapter in C Burger *et al* (eds), *Cultivating Missional Change: The Future of Missional Churches and Missional Theology* (Wellington, South Africa: Biblecor, 2017) pp 306–319.

5. The best-known practitioners of this tradition are the Tavistock Institute of Human Relations; see http://www.tavinstitute.org/who-we-are/

6. Edwin Friedman, *Generation to Generation: Family Process in Church and Synagogue* (New York: Guilford, 1985).

7. *ibid*, p 9.

8. *ibid*, p 23.

9. *Forming the Missional Church, op cit*, p 8.

10. Friedman, *op cit*, p 27, my emphasis.

11. As Pat often says to those who blithely think it is easy to maintain a non-anxious presence, 'The only truly non-anxious presence I know is a dead one!'

12. Friedman, *op cit*, p 35.

13. For example Bridge Builders, run by the peace-building Mennonite Church.

14. Vega Z Roberts, 'The Organization of Work: Contributions from Open Systems Theory' in Vega Z Roberts and Anton Obholzer, *The Unconscious at Work: Individual and Organizational Stress in the Human Services* (London: Routledge, 1994) pp 28–38.

15. Downloaded from Wikimedia Commons (more complex versions are available and worth exploring): https://upload.wikimedia.org/wikipedia/commons/7/77/OpenSystemRepresentation.svg (accessed 07 February 2019).

16. See Paul Sparks, Tim Soerens and Dwight J Friesen, *The New Parish: How Neighborhood Churches are Transforming Mission, Discipleship and Community* (Downers Grove, IL: IVP, 2014) and https://parishcollective.org/

17. Patrick R Keifert, *Welcoming the Stranger: A Public Theology of Worship and Evangelism* (Minneapolis, MN: Fortress, 1992).

18 Roberts, *op cit*, p 29.

19 Roberts, *op cit*, p 29.

20 Roberts, *op cit*, pp 37–38.

21 P G Hiebert, *Transforming Worldviews: An Anthropological Understanding of How People Change* (Grand Rapids, MI: Baker, 2008) p 36.

22 I add this in here to show how the theory crosses over disciplines and would therefore seem, I conjecture, to be a part of God's good created order.

23 R Heifetz, A Grashow and M Linsky, *The Practice of Adaptive Leadership: Tools and Tactics for Changing your Organization and the World* (Boston, MA: Harvard Business Press, 2009) pp 7–8.

24 M Paterson, 'Discipled by praxis: soul and role in context,' *Practical Theology* (2019), DOI: 10.1080/1756073X.2018.1562689

25 Heifetz, *op cit*, p 156.

26 Roberts, *op cit*, p 30.

27 Roberts, *op cit*, p 31.

28 As argued in Ian Cowley, *The Contemplative Response: Leadership and Ministry in a Distracted Culture* (Oxford: BRF, 2019).

29 See Harold Miller, *Finding a Personal Rule of Life* (Grove Spirituality booklet S8).

30 Adrian Chatfield and Nigel Rooms, *Soul Friendship: A Practical Theology of Spiritual Direction* (London: Canterbury Press, 2019).

31 For more on this see particularly Patrick R Keifert, *Welcoming the Stranger, op cit.*

32 This typology is helpfully used in the Cynefin, or simple model of decision-making innovated by David Snowden and company. See David J Snowden and Mary E Boone, *Harvard Business Review*, November 2007, pp 69–76. See also https://cognitive-edge.com/

33 Barry M Johnson, *Polarity Management: Identifying and Managing Unsolvable Problems* (Amherst, MA: HRD Press, 1992).

34 Roy Oswald and Barry Johnson, *Managing Polarities in Congregations: Eight Keys for Thriving Faith Communities* (London: Rowman and Littlefield, 2009).